Phulkari

Harman Kaur

ISBN: 1775319008

ISBN-13: 978-1775319009

For my heart

CONTENTS

ACKNOWLEDGMENTS

This book took a whole parivaar to get here.

To my parents, Gursewak Singh and Kulwinder Kaur: thank you for giving me life and supporting me the whole way. Thank you for making my dreams your dreams.

To my brother, Harsimran Singh: not many people can call their brother their best friend. Thank you for constantly listening to my plans and being my rock.

To Mana and Param: my two favourite people who support everything I do and make fun of me to keep me humble.

To Prabh Dhillon: thank you for being a massive force behind *Phulkari*. You contributed way more than just the amazing illustrations to it and we both know I would have been a mess without you.

To Gurpreet Kaur Sangha: thank you for being my biggest fan and my best friend. You have always believed in me, even when I have stopped believing in myself.

To Jasmin Kaur: thank you for inspiring me to be a better writer, for your friendship and for your words. You brought the sisterhood into my life that I had always dreamed of.

To Ranvir Singh and Darshveer Singh: thank you for always bringing cuddles and laughter into my life whenever the writing became too draining. Bhuji loves you so much.

And lastly, to my Guru, the weaver. All of these words are yours; I am simply the messenger. Thank you for blessing me with the ability to carry on the Sikh legacy of poetry.

FOREWORD

On June 24, 2017, I asked for Guru Ji's blessings before I officially started writing *Phulkari*, during the bhog of a 15-day sehaj paath. Nine months later (coincidentally), at the end of March, the book was finished and I emotionally prepared myself to share it with the world. I'm not going to lie and say that the last 9 months were easy, but the worst part came when I was almost finished. I began crumbling with self-doubt and regretted even thinking that I could write a book. After talking with my loved ones, however, I realized that I had a story to tell and anyone who wanted to know it could pick up *Phulkari* to read it. I was not telling the story of *all* Sikhs or Panjabis or women, but there would be stories in this book that someone out there could relate to or learn from. Stories that someone out there needed to read just as much as I needed to write them. So, I carried on writing and now the book you are holding in your hands is just as much yours as it is mine. Thank you for believing in me.

I will not translate
my experience
define my trauma
justify my femininity
or limit my creativity;

if the poem does not send
an ache of familiarity
throughout your body
on the first read

it was not written for you.

I.

The Fraying

Every so often
I let someone get
too close
they tear me
right at the seams
and this is
how the fraying
begins

The past still wakes me up

some nights

uninvited, uncalled for,

unnecessary,

but not unusual.

It does not leave

until the sun comes up

and I ponder

why it is that

I dismiss the hurting as

dwelling in the past

when the memories

have made a home in my lungs.

When the pain is present

now

There are no poems, no words heavy enough
to break what is inside me. I am two parts
too much and one part not enough.
    Unbalanced.
Determined to break down your walls
whilst putting up my own. Getting to
the root of my trauma. Staying there.
Getting lost there.
Forgetting to come back up for air.
I am resilient but I am not. Hardened by the
same thing that softens me. Weakened by
the very thing that empowers me.
I am a tangle of contradictions
    a mess of mistakes.
Masking love with anger. Mistaking anger
for love. I am powerful in the same breath
that I am not. Breaking promises with
the same sureness that I make them.
Breaking people. Loving people.
Do I need to break myself to love?
I am two parts too much and one part
not enough. Unbalanced. *Human.*

Reminder

Do not destroy them just because
someone once destroyed you.

I learned silence from my father;

this is the only way he was ever allowed to grieve.

I inherited my mother's rage;

this is the only way she was ever heard.

A culture of silence has turned

our fathers into men

with storms

churning inside

of them

and

eyes

that are

not allowed

to rain

You always knew how to leave

but never quite learned

the art of staying gone

and I

a mountain of a woman

crumbled every time

you returned

I allow him to step out

and step right in

as if I am a revolving door

and not

a woman once made of walls

I must learn how to
differentiate
between people
as if they are water
and air

I need both

but only one is safe
inside these two lungs

I know you tried to wear your heart on your sleeve.

Tore your walls down for one person.

Allowed yourself to let them in.

Unlocked all of the doors.

I know it broke you.

Trust me.

It's broken me, too.

Lost yourself in losing them.

It made you lock all the doors.

Build up all the walls you had torn down.

I now know why you wear a sleeve over your heart.

Interpretations of a highly complex woman

I hope the one who comes next will
read me differently than you did.

Marathons

He tells me I am good at running

that I move as if I can outrun pain,

as if I have ever been successful.

(I have not.)

He says running makes me weak

but would a weak person be able

to run this long?

(I think not.)

My lungs have adapted to carrying me

for miles, but at some point or another

they beg me to stop.

(I do not.)

When I am convinced that I have

travelled far enough, I wait for the pain

to leave my body.

(It does not, it never does)

You see

I put my heart and soul into everything I do
and everyone I meet. This is why it is always
so hard to let go; I allow them to become
a part of me. I have never known how to
interact without opening myself up, never been
interested in the idea of walls or borders.
So, I live and exist with pieces of me scattered
across 3 countries and 10 cities.

A part of me rests in Panjab. Fragments scattered
across New York. Pieces lost in San Francisco.

I am never fully present standing before you.

My mistake was that

I tried to grow into

new skin without

completely

    shedding

        myself

           of

              you

Selfless people
carry the heaviest
of hearts

they listen
to your worries and
regrets

become the place
where you finally put down
all the baggage
you have been carrying

take on all your burdens
but never give you theirs in return

I found you

at the peak of summer

the sun

a witness to all

our memories

and as the days got

shorter

and the leaves changed

colour

so did you

you came to me

a season disguised

as a lifetime

It takes more strength than I will ever have to walk away from a love that is not working anymore.

There are parts of me
that still mourn your absence

sometimes in tears
mostly in forced smiles

If I told you about

the darkness

inside of me

would you still

look at me

like I am the Sun?

Reminder

Perhaps there is a reason why you still ache for them after all this time. You keep waiting for the grieving to end, but have you ever allowed yourself to start?

I know you keep yourself occupied, keep yourself moving, because if you stop you will have time to think and when you think, your mind always wanders to what you are running from. The *hurting*. How can you outrun something that is a part of you, though, and how do you separate yourself from it? How can you tire yourself out, avoid facing the pain and call that healing? Don't you know that this is only the *fraying*?

II.

The Weaver

Take me apart
sew me back together

what more can I do
but accept it

when you are the weaver
and I
a mere cloth

Every time I take a breath

I wish to breathe out
a part of me
(*wahe*)

so I can breathe in
a part of you
(*guru*)

Like a leaf falling
off of a tree   I
have come into this world

pushed along by
a wind of illusion, I   am
twirling and floating

failing to realize
that I was   broken
away from you

but this separation
will change me   without
a warning;

I will turn
whatever colours   you
please and *crumble*.

- An Ode to Pavana Reddy's 'my heart blossoms for you'

ਪ੍ਰਨਾਮ ਸ਼ਹੀਦਾਂ ਨੂੰ

This sikhi came with a price

that I did not have to pay.

I admit I tried to bury my pain

but it grew just like a seed

so I set it aflame

because you see

when my people

cremate

we read gurbani

and learn to

accept the will

of the guru

and this how

I finally found my peace

Stories of Panjab, 1984

When the news of the attack on Darbaar Sahib reaches the ears of Kulwinder Kaur and her friends, they recognize it for what it is: an attempt to erase and silence their people. So when they wake up for school the next morning, they replace their blue chunnis with kesri, and wear a symbol of azaadi and shahaadat on their heads as a reminder to the state: *We still exist. You will not erase us.* When their teacher calls for everyone to stand up and sing along to the Indian national anthem, their hearts beat courageously for their kaum and their mouths sing: *deh shiva bar mohe ehai shubh kar man te kab hu na taro*. Refusing to be silenced, this is how they create a revolution in a tiny village in Panjab. The flame that Jaswant Singh Khalra would later immortalize is lit many times as a challenge to a whole nation.

Darbaar Sahib

Understand that
what you see
as a gold-covered
tourist destination

was the heart of
my people
before gold ever
touched its walls

I am thankful for the grief
that drives me away from
temporary things
and leads me
to you

If he asks for your love
remind him that
you had to learn
how to live and breathe a love
that understands
you are a sovereign being
the kind of love
that has the courage
to let *you* decide
the way Guru Gobind Singh
gave Ajit Singh his blessings
to walk into the arms of death
tell him there is a love
that embraces you
without wishing to
conquer or
suffocate
one that has the forgiveness
to tear a bedava right
before your eyes
a love that cannot
help but see
the divine in
every living being
like Bhai Ghanaiya Ji
a love that is not
passive
a revolutionary love
when he offers you his love
make him remember
the word shahaadat

remind him that there
have been more sacrifices made
than the strands of hair on his head
more blood given
than that which flows
through his veins
and this
this is the only love
you have known since you
took your first breath
a love that has been there
before you and him
even existed
and will continue living
when you are gone
so when he asks for
your love
tell him of the love
of the gurus
of the chaar sahibzade
of Bibi Bhani and
Mata Gujri Ji
recount the sakhis
of Guru Nanak and
Bhai Mardana ji
and then

ask him
if he will learn

You and I crumble
before the same father

tell me why I should
carry your fragile honour

when it is the guru
that puts me back together

and not you

Reminder

Do not curse yourself for having hope:
to have hope is to trust in your guru.

Kaur

is liberation
from the systems
and hierarchies
of the world

a declaration
that you and I
are one

I am not above you
or beneath you

I stand *beside* you

so if you know
of the name
I carry
leave all of your
misconceptions
where I left mine

at the feet of my guru
every time
I fell

Brother
if your songs of revolution
forget to pay tribute
to kaurs

neglect to mention
the names of
Bibi Manjit Kaur Babbar
and
Bibi Resham Kaur

omit the women
who put the panth
before themselves

you have missed half the revolution

To my father, Guru Gobind Singh

How can I ever think
I am worth nothing
when you gave up
four diamonds and
felt no loss because

you still had me

Being a child of
Guru Gobind Singh
and falling apart
does not make me
unworthy;

even glass
forged from fire
breaks sometimes

I think I must have
met my guru
once or twice
at least
because
some people
came at exactly
the right time
as blessings
too perfect
too real to just be

coincidences

ਬੰਦੀ ਛੋੜ / *Bandi Chhod*

My guru refused to be freed
without fifty-two kings
and sometimes I think I am
one of them

imprisoned and miserable
in a world ruled by maya

until my guru found me
took me by the hand
and *set me free*

My dear friend

1430 angs are read in celebration of my birth.
(you were there from the beginning)

When I turn 7, we buy a new house and I do not
understand what ma means when she says
'guru ji is coming home'
1430 angs worth of love grace our new home.

I am 10 and my fingers graze 1430 angs
for the first time as I learn how to pronounce
the truth.

My happiness and my grief lead me back to
these 1430 angs. I always find my answers.

When I have breathed my last
it is 1430 angs that will perform my final rites.
(you will be there until the end)

Jithai jaae behai mera satguru
so thaan suhaava raam raajae
(Wherever my true guru sits,
that place is beautiful, O king)

- a sudden realization that if
I let go of my doubts
I will make room for you
in my heart, mind, and soul

and they, too, will turn beautiful.

When they ask me
how I found my guru
and fell in love

I tell them

I fell asleep
each night
to the sound of
mool mantar

I found my guru
in the voice
of my mother

I think of Maha Singh
laying in the lap of
Guru Gobind Singh,
asking for forgiveness
with his last few breaths

and I realize
my guru has always
sent a Mai Bhago
to bring me back, too.

Reminder

Learn to trust in your instincts:
your guru is trying to tell you something.

My people cannot
ramble off
textbook definitions
of
oppression
or
police brutality
or
state-sponsored violence

but they have looked
persecution in the eye

protested the khaki uniforms
that left them bare

and watched as the word genocide
was ripped over and over again
from their throats –

I ask you
does this not count for something?

Dear guru ji

when getting out of bed gets too hard
I find myself running to your darbaar

and when you hear my cries and ease my pain
I lose myself in happiness and forget you again

I feel like I must make a confession
that I am left with only one question:

Am I only your Sikh when it's convenient?

A Consolation

If you feel empty because they have left you, it's okay.
Sometimes, we become their habits and they realize
that too late. Other times, they become ours. When the
void they leave behind becomes unbearable, let yourself
break completely. Put yourself together with baani – there
is no glue stronger than that. Fill yourself with the
realization that this human life is temporary and so are
the people we come to love. Remember that it is important
to love people, but that does not mean they own you.
It also means that you do not own them, so when they
leave because they need to, you have to let them go.
Finally, surrender yourself to your guru, who has been
there before they arrived and will remain after they leave,
and you will never have to fear love again.

I have learned to walk with
my head held high
even when my circumstances
have tried to push it down

my head belongs to
my guru

how can I let it bow
to my doubts and fears

I know it seems like your ardaas
is nothing but a whisper among
the cries of a suffering world

but your guru will always hear
your guru will always *listen*

ੲੲਤਾ / *Ekta*

My first experience with death comes in May of 2004. I am 8.
I learn that Bibi Reena Kaur has passed away and I do not
know what this means, but I *feel* it. My small little body feels
the distress and I bury my face in my bed and think about
what death even means. The whole panth grieves for our
family members, Bhai Charanjit Singh, Bhai Parminder Singh,
and Bibi Reena Kaur, and celebrates them with barsees to this
day. Harsimran Singh leaves this world in January of 2018 and
I see again what it means when we say the panth is a family.
That regardless of everything that divides us and turns us
against each other, we carry each other through the hardest of
times. A sea of blue. An army. Family. And *this* is what ekta
looks like.

III.

Thread & Needle

For my children I will practice
what my mother breathed into me
she reminded me that my elders
left a land of five rivers
and brought the name
outsider to this new land
and I must honour this

She said

If living here makes you take an
axe to your roots and strip
away at your identity until
your mother(land)
does not recognize her own child
remember that you will have
become an outsider everywhere

I hold onto her words

The same way she weaved this
into me, like *thread and*
needle, I vow to teach
my children of the people
of the unceded land on which
they reside. They will learn
to honour them, too.

  - From Panjab to unceded Sto:lo land

ਮਾਪੇ / Maapeh

You worked the soil
of a new country

sun beating down
on broken backs and
dirt stuck in fingernails

planted seeds that cost
every thing you had

and from this
I harvested my dreams

An open letter to the desi art community

I refuse to use the struggles
of my immigrant parents
to entertain those
who will never understand

This one is for the mothers who carried us
for nine months inside their wombs and
for a lifetime outside of it. Brown mothers.
Immigrant mothers. Broken-english speaking
mothers. Up at the crack of dawn to work
jobs that break their back mothers.
The women who learned how to wear
jeans when we made a face at their
salwaars. Resilient women. Powerful women.
Panjabi women. Sikh women. Women with
ungrateful children. Privileged children.
Building our dreams on the backs of their
mothers children. *This one is for them.*

My father's accent is enough
to make you wrinkle your nose
in disgust   but you have never
had to balance a second language
on your tongue and even if you
think you could   remember that
my mother tongue makes sounds
that leave english at a loss for letters

When I ask my mother what she misses the most
about Panjab, she says to me

I cry, laugh, and get angry in my maa boli.
These emotions roll off my tongue in the
language that is natural to me. Here, my feelings
must be translated. In Panjab, they are understood.

I miss being understood.

I realize my people have been lost in translation.

ਮਾਂ ਬੋਲੀ / *Maa boli*

We call it our mother tongue
yet it is treated as a foreigner
inside our mouths

it shows up at our doorstep
and no one invites it in

tries to instill pride
but all we feel is shame

knows the secrets of the world
though we call it uneducated

when did our mother become
a complete *stranger?*

ਆਪਣੇ ੧ / *Apne* I

Seeing an unfamiliar Panjabi face
on television still causes my mother to
beam with pride because she says excitedly

'that person is an *apna*'
(that person is *our own*)

our mother tongue always keeps us connected;
we are each other's before we ever meet

ਆਪਣੇ ੨ / *Apne* II

But what happens
what do you do
when you are
disowned
by the ones
you call *apneh*

the ones you
call your own

My father's dilemma

One foot is in Panjab
planted deep in soil
roots attached to the khet
like kanak

the other here
in a new country
scraping against
concrete roads

no wonder I keep falling down:
life won't let me keep balance.

The immigrant success story

The immigrant narratives
seem to focus only
on the accomplishments
of newcomers
in a country that tries to
strip away our hardships
and feed them back to us
as success stories

what of the unfinished stories
left back home?

My parents have almost
set themselves on fire
to put out the flames
that surround me

ਦਾਦੀ ਜੀ / *Daadi Ji*

I have never believed that exaggerated metaphors
should be applied to love. Love has never told me
I must move mountains or capture stars from the
night sky.   Love is no metaphor.
How unfair, then, that I literally had to cross
oceans to get to you and *I couldn't.*

ਆਪਣੇ 3 / *Apne* III

An 18 year old boy is referred to as a man in the headlines.
The body has not been identified yet, but gang violence is
a common occurrence in the city of Abbotsford.

The newspapers always present opinions filled with stories
of immigrant parents who spoil their sons. No mention
is made of the violence that goes on inside the four walls
of Panjabi households. The silencing. The abuse.
No mention of the immigrant struggle. The late-night
shifts. The presentation of toxic masculinity. The bottled-up
rage. The depression. No cultural context, whatsoever.

My mother tells me about the shooting as soon as I walk
in through the door. I tell her I already know. She asks me
if I know who died. I tell her I probably do.

You see, I do not know if the victim is a Panjabi boy yet
but white comments under Facebook articles seem to
know already. And while they make demands for deportations
of 'gangsters' who are born and raised in Canada, my heart
sinks as a name is released. I recognize it. A face comes to mind
as soon as I hear it.

And so we grieve. For the mother of the boy. For the family.
For the community. For ourselves. The boy was an apna.
He was our own, after all

ਪੰਜਾਬ

She is the land
of five rivers

but Panjab
is kept thirsty

Everything is in a name

A sunflower
is neither the sun
nor just a flower

so why do you allow
them to call you
just a fragment
of who you are

why cater to their
refusal to learn
how to pronounce
when you can
sound out dictionaries
filled with english
words

when you can recognize
the 'r' in colonel
though it is not present
and
have spent years
with them in classes
memorizing names
of complicated
chemical compounds

and I ask you

if they can pronounce
sodium carbonate decahydrate
then how is Jaspreet
or Harsimran
or Gurjeet
so strenuous

so arduous

so onerous

there is meaning
in your name
learn it
own it
live it

a sunflower
is neither the sun
nor just any flower

do not let them
address you by only
a portion
of who you are
either

Decolonizing

I have learned that the point is
not to figure out who you are
but who you are not

but who I am to make a fuss
over reclaiming the bindi
when it was never mine
to reclaim anyways

you see
I cannot drown myself
in tikkas and earrings of gold
to reclaim my identity

will not adorn myself in
my mother's anand karaj outfit
and call it decolonizing
when Panjabi Sikh bodies
have been tortured and silenced
for centuries now

I reclaim my identity
by wearing my dastaar
unapologetically

by refusing to stay silent
even when silence
is all that is expected of me

and this is how I take back
my body

There is a phrase in Panjabi that comforts me: *dukh vandauna*. It literally means 'to divide and share the pain'. It makes sense, does it not? We are given all this pain – how else will we survive if we do not cut it to pieces?

Let go. Breathe. You do not have to hurt alone.

So, you made a mistake. The ones you have hurt will forgive you at their own pace. You might take even longer to forgive yourself, but keep in mind that in your mother tongue, Panjabi, one of the words for mistake is the same as the word that means "to forget": *bhul*.

Is that not beautiful? How forgiving our mother tongue is, that she recognizes you made a mistake because you forgot who you were for a moment. Or two. Or many. You forgot how much you loved the person you hurt. Forgot your morals. Your guru. And this is okay. We all forget.

So, the next time someone tells you that Panjabi is rough and unsophisticated, tell them that there can be nothing as kind. As soft. As merciful.

IV.

Silk

I aspire to be

a woman of silk;

soft and strong

at the same time

I do not mind
that the brown-skinned
girl with the turban
is never seen in any
poems or movies,

they never manage
to get it right anyways;

I will write my own story.

Brown girl

in your fight
to taste freedom
do not let
your mother
starve

Your mother has been taught
to be an echo and shadow
of your father

do not raise your voice
against her
because you were not
taught the same.

Resistance

I will not allow you to turn

my body
into my own prison

my womanhood
into my own shackles.

my existence
into a crime

Can you imagine having
the body of a woman?
always covered too much
or not enough

Reminder

This body is too much my own
to carry anybody else's honour.

If 'purity' is how we
insist on measuring
the worth of our
daughters, we might
come to find that
our sons are worth
nothing

Hide
cover
silence yourself

until you barely exist

and then maybe
just maybe
the men will stop raping.

One day I might carry
a child inside of me

my body could become
a home

but I must confess

the thought of being
a home
for nine months
is bewildering

I have not felt
at home
in my own body
ever since I
transitioned
into womanhood

how do I provide
a sanctuary
for another?

I often wonder   if this body
could not bear a child would I
still be deemed woman enough?
Human enough? If a woman carries
the desire for a child in her heart
but never carries one in her womb,
is she worth anything?

If I should have a daughter, I will tell her that
there are many different types of love – romantic
is not the only one worth holding on to.

I will teach her that romantic love is not the only
love that heals; she will find a sanctuary in her guru,
solace in her father's arms, and a lover in herself.

Just the same, I will remind her that romantic
love is not the only type of love that destroys.

I will watch helplessly on the days her self-love
crumbles. I will remember that my biggest regret
was the loss of a friend. I will never deny that I am
just as capable of breaking her heart, too.

If I should have a daughter, I will let her choose.
What point is there to love if it is not freeing?
If it does not allow you to breathe?

The little girl I used to be

the teenager I want to forget

and the woman I want to be

I carry all three with me
as a reminder of who I am

I think of the woman
I came from and
the countless women
before her
made to shrink
into shadows
and taught to speak
only
when spoken to
and while reminding
myself to be louder
and take up more space
I realize *I* could be
their silence
coming back for
revenge

Somewhere
between the red flags
his forced apologies
and empty promises

are the echoes of
your mother's silence
begging you to *leave*.

Mother,
do not raise me
with the thought of
giving me away

I
am not your burden
of unwanted fruit
that must be raised
until I ripen

I
was not made to just
fill the stomachs
of generations
whilst I starve

Mother,
allow me to grow
and do not worry
about spoiled fruit

When he tells you he owns you

when he says
you are mine
as if you are some ordinary object

remember that you are the ocean
that no one can lay claim to

you are the sky
so vast and beautiful

and what human could possibly master you?

Sister

we both shine like
Sun and Moon
taking turns
to light up the sky
          but
how did I forget
the world
only counts down
to an *eclipse*

There will come a day when
the words will not form and
the writing will fail to offer
any solace

put down the pen

immerse yourself in the
poetry
of women of colour

and marvel at how
one way or another
it is words that have saved you
once again

I admit I tried to change, but over time I am learning that I do not have to unbecome the woman you once loved to erase you. I do not have to unlearn the ways in which I love because they remind me of you. I will not retrain myself to stifle my laughter at the things you also found amusing. I refuse to behave, look, and sound different, to become a completely different woman because of you.

You might have loved the woman I am, but so do I. And she will *not* follow you out of my life, too

V.

DYE

I remember sitting in the back of a car in Panjab, intently watching a man dye a chunni in front of his shop.
I watched as he took a white chunni and plunged it into the dye. When he finally took it out, it was completely red. Permanently. No trace of white left.

This is what you have done to me with your love
and I have not been the same since.

Until now
I had only felt the rain

with you I met a storm

Even 5000 miles of distance will
not keep us apart if your name
is on my lips in every prayer.

Timezones

The moon
and I share
stories
about you
it rises
on your side
of the world
first
only so
it can
race back
to me
every night
and console
my heart

These days
my love letters
look more like apology notes

all the ways in which
I know how to say
I love you
come flowing out
in remorse

some say that
love tastes the best
when it is served
with a side of reciprocity

I say

just loving you
is enough
to ease this hunger

Perhaps one day
years from now

we will run into each other again
in some crowded place

and break because
we can still spot each other
among thousands of people

There is something about
the way you smile

I have made a home in it

I see the roof collapse
and get drenched in rain
every time it disappears

I am convinced the sun
bows its head in awe
every single night
and rises in the morning
bright and early
just to catch a glimpse
of you

There is a love that will bring you
down to your knees with prayers
full of gratitude, because this love is
a *privilege*. An honour.
You will take it for granted because
it is always present and
this is how you will lose it.

Reminder

Love is what brings two people together
it is not what makes them stay there

You are used to
a loud kind of love.
This one is quiet.

He does not tell you
he loves you
multiple times a day.
He does it once. Just once.

He says he was never
good with putting
his feelings into words
but he swears he is trying

and sometimes
you will get fed up
and tell yourself
you deserve better

but the love
although it is quiet
is real
and that makes it
enough.

I,
a tsu-
nami of
a woman,
fell like rain
drops for
you

The joy always
comes in colours.

Some days
I am a blank canvas
or a faded photograph

but today my love
I am a *phulkari*.

When we first met
I realized
the souls of lovers
do not finally meet

they are simply
returning to one
another

The story of the Sun
and the Moon
and the love they share
has been told for ages
(but that is not our story)

you may be the Sun

but I am the Sky
that lights up in
your presence

and plunges into
a deep darkness
in your absence

I can't bring myself to regret
any of the decisions
I have made in this lifetime

because somehow

they all led me to you

When I tell you that you are my strength
it means I have invested in you so much
of my love and courage – so much of *me*,
that when something breaks inside of me
I look to you as a reminder of *who I am*.

VI.

Flowerwork

What is life

but the flowerwork
on a phulkari

dyed with colour
and made of silk
stitched by the weaver
with thread and needle

the joy
the sorrows
the triumphs
the losses

all weaved together
to make up who you are
and who you will become

The pain taught me
how to write
and
the writing taught me
how to heal

I will not break myself open again

to show you where you hurt me.

After breaking
all you will want
is for every wound
to close

(but what is healing
if not revisiting
confronting
and letting go of
that which broke you
in the first place)

to find
that the healing
sometimes hurts
more than
the breaking

I housed the pain
 inside of me
for months and
(unbeknownst to me)
it grew until I could
hide it no longer

*My mother always taught me
that letting go is hardest when
you wait too long.*

So, brace yourself.
Close your eyes.
Remember how to breathe.

Releasing the trauma
is like
giving birth.　　　It hurts.

And then it *doesn't.*

You tell me
muscles must tear apart
to rebuild stronger
than before
so I know
it must be the same
for the heart.

- dedicated to Gurpreet Kaur Sangha

When you left
flowers began
to bloom
inside my mind

and then I understood

I know they made
a home
of your lungs

a bittersweet reminder
accompanying
every breath

tell me about how
the breathing
comes easier

how you no longer
gasp for air

now that they
(and their baggage)
have vacated

Reminder

Although the happiness tends to disappear
after a while, *so does the pain.*

Sometimes I wish I did not feel so deeply
and could be drained of all these emotions
because they leave me feeling weakened
and then I think of the ocean who is called
that because she carries more than any
lake or river ever could and I realize this
is not my weakness, it is my *strength*.

Somewhere along the way
we kill off versions of ourselves.
Softer
quieter versions.
Passive
fragile versions.

Do not mourn them.

They may not have survived
what we have lived through.

There is something about being alone
that calms me. Even while the anguish
of letting go consumes me.

I remind myself over and over again
(like a prayer) that I finally own every
single part of me. I belong only and
wholly to myself. Alone (all own).

I love others without boundaries
so why should my self-love come
with restrictions? I must love myself
in the same way. Choose myself over
and over again. Find that balance. Love
in a way that is selfless, but not in a way
that will leave me starving.

I see us
wrapping rebellion (in obedience)
storing rage (in silence)
how long can we keep
trying to contain the storms
within
for fear that those
around us will get
drenched
in the downpour
I say
let out a thunderous roar
that breaks
      the sky
        in half
and the smell after a rainfall?
- *that is but the scent of freedom*

It turns out I was the sun all along;
your vision was just clouded

He thinks I have outgrown him so
I remind him that my own body

has always pushed me out to make
space for others. How I have

exhausted my lungs and bent my
spine. Broken my back over and

over again, without keeping record
of what love has cost me. If this

is what love is supposed to look
like, I have given it all away and

left none for myself. So when he
accuses me of being distant, I tell

him that I am not outgrowing *him*;
I am just finally growing into *myself*.

I realize now that the restlessness I feel inside of me
is a desire to be *free*

You are a body that contains waves
of emotions. Do not stand frozen
as life continues moving around you.

Learn from the ocean the art of moving;
you will need it when winter arrives.

I have too many dreams
to be losing any sleep over you.

The poem will not always be your sanctuary

rhymes and syllables
will not always provide relief
as soon as pen is put to paper

when the lines destroy
your comfort zone

only then will the words set you free.

If they should become undeserving of your kindness,
do not allow it to leave you, even if the hurting almost
turns you cold with apathy. On some days, your kindness
will be the only source of warmth you will find

- hold onto it for yourself.

I look back at my past selves
the way a mother looks
at her disobedient child;

eyes full of disappointment
and heart full of forgiveness

Here you are, waiting for the universe
to give you a sign, when there is a universe
inside of you that is waiting for a signal
only *you* can give.

An afterthought

Death is not the colour black. Nor is it white. Death is the neela my people wear with pride. The beautiful browns of our eyes and skin, a declaration that we carry the sun with us wherever we go. The kesri we proudly raise against a light blue sky. Death is yellows and blues and greens. The silver glints of our kirpaans and karas. Death is laal and gulabi and jahmni. The flash of colour I will see before I close these eyes forever. To have lived such a colourful life is not something I will allow to be mourned in blacks and whites

- it will be celebrated *in a rainbow of phulkaris.*

Harman Kaur is a writer and spoken word artist from Abbotsford, BC, Canada. Her work delves into the complexities that come with being a Panjabi Sikh woman. She has travelled across Canada and the US to perform her work and to facilitate workshops. You can find her work on Instagram (@__harmankaur) or visit her website: www.harmankaur.ca.

Prabhsimran Singh Dhillon is an artist, designer and creative director from Surrey, BC, Canada. He is also a humanitarian who finds happiness in serving others. You can find Prabh's work on Instagram (@prbdlln) or learn more about him on his website: www.prbdlln.com